for women

like
book ™

a gift for:

Kelda

from:

_____

year:

2012

message:

_____

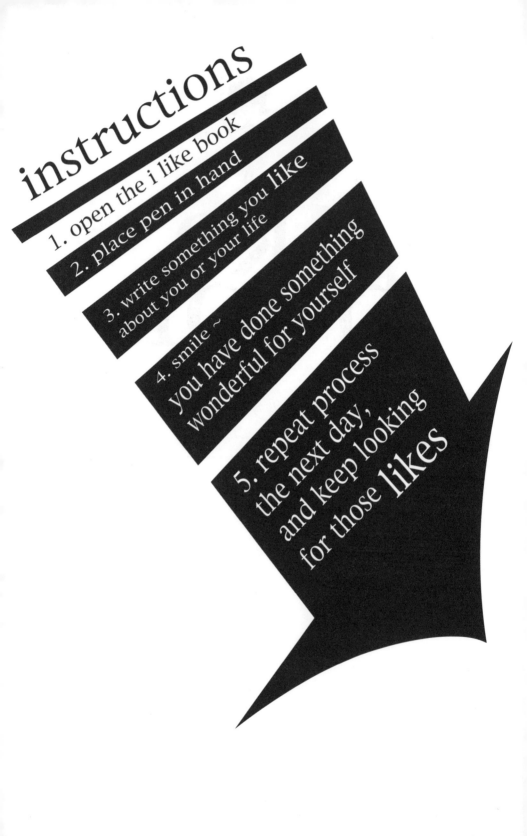

instructions

1. open the i like book

2. place pen in hand

3. write something you like about you or your life

4. smile ~ you have done something wonderful for yourself

5. repeat process the next day, and keep looking for those likes

because **you** are an original

an **i like book** for women? **yes!** it's time to celebrate **you**. treat yourself to a moment each day appreciating the little and big **likes** in your life. the **i like book** for women allows you to feel **peace, inspiration** and **inner freedom**. start now and **feel the power of positivity in your life.**

like your life to a **new level**

experience a **journey of self discovery**

it is **all about you**...and that is **ok**

"i highly recommend this book to all women. i feel refreshed and it puts me in a positive state of mind. i **guarantee** you will love it."

—rebekah

"this absolutely **adorable** book has allowed me to see the **simple things** in life that i would never have noticed otherwise. thank you."

—sarah

"i feel this book was designed just for me. i am more centered and peaceful when i write my thoughts down about **my life.**"

—mary

like your life

like book

for women

because **you** are an original

created by
meredith looney

design & layout by
jani duncan smith, it girl design, llc

our guarantee:

we believe so strongly in the message of the i like book that we are making this quality guarantee to you. if for any reason you are disappointed, we will refund the purchase price of the book.

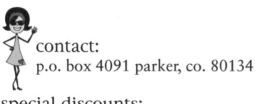

contact:
p.o. box 4091 parker, co. 80134

special discounts:

for information on wholesale pricing please contact us at 888.737.like (5453) or visit our website www.theilikebook.com

1st edition. ©2012 lucky looney llc. all rights reserved.
printed in the usa. i like books are eco-friendly, made with 30% post-consumer recycled fiber, soy based ink and acid free paper.

 dedication

this book is dedicated to all women. may you find **inspiration, inner peace** and **happiness** in your journey of self-discovery. like your life.

Meredith Looney

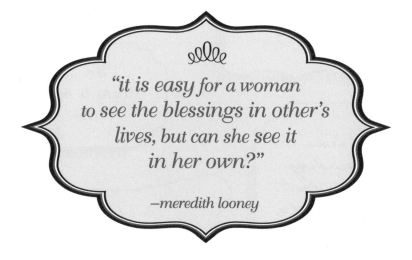

"it is easy for a woman to see the blessings in other's lives, but can she see it in her own?"

—meredith looney

i like ...
warm coffee
in the morning

i like ...
meeting my
friends for
lunch

i like ...
that i've exercised
3 days in a row

i like ...
that i slept good
last night

i like ...
that i woke
up to
sunshine
and birds
chirping

i like ...
enjoying time
alone

i like ...
trying a new
recipe

i like ...
reading
the last
page of a
good book
twice

i like ...
when my favorite song
comes on the radio

October
month

1 i like ... _____

2 i like ... _____

3 i like ... _____

4 i like ... _____

5 i like ... _____

6 i like ... _____

7 i like ... _____

i like...waking up with a good attitude

"life is like riding a bicycle, in order to keep your balance **you must keep moving."**

—albert einstein

October 2012
month

i like ... _____
8 _____
_____
_____

i like ... _____
9 _____
_____
_____

i like ... _____
10 _____
_____
_____

i like ... _____
11 _____
_____
_____

i like ... Lazy days, Can't wait for
12 the weekend.
_____
_____

i like ... the changing colors on the
13 trees, the cool air in the morning, and
warm arms holding me when I wake
up. I feel so loved !! Thank you Mario

i like ... Sleeping in... taking naps...
14 and taking time out to spend
with my daughter
_____

i like...sunshine

"there is a time when *you* just have to stick your feet out the window."

—brooke

October 2012
month

i like ... Special moments with my daughter. We danced to country music, and fell down laughing. I love her so much, so much fun!

i like ...

i like ...

i like ...

i like ...

i like ...

i like ...

i like...me!

_____ month

i like ... _____
22 _____
_____

i like ... _____
23 _____
_____

i like ... _____
24 _____
_____

i like ... _____
25 _____
_____

i like ... _____
26 _____
_____

i like ... _____
27 _____
_____

i like ... _____
28 _____
_____

i like...being creative

dream ✺ sieze the day ✺ reach the sky ✺ live today ✺ continue to climb ✺ say "yes" to life ✺ believe in you ✺ be different ✺ do the undoable ✺ embrace your dreams ✺ find the power within ✺ do your best ✺ make someone smile ✺ be original ✺ create your destiny ✺ be kind ✺ laugh at yourself ✺ find your journey ✺ dream

_____ month

i like ... _____
29 _____
_____
_____

i like ... _____
30 _____
_____
_____

i like ... _____
31 _____
_____
_____

i like…taking naps

_____ month

1 i like ... _____
_____
_____
_____

2 i like ... _____
_____
_____

3 i like ... _____
_____
_____

4 i like ... _____
_____
_____

5 i like ... _____
_____
_____
_____

6 i like ... _____
_____
_____
_____

7 i like ... _____
_____
_____
_____

i like...reading a good book

begin
each day
with thoughts
that bring out
the best
in you

today i will * *yes i can* * *i am grateful* * *i am loveable* * *i believe in myself* * *i can make a difference* *

month

i like ...

8

i like ...

9

i like ...

10

i like ...

11

i like ...

12

i like ...

13

i like ...

14

i like…good hair days

"because every picture,
has a story to tell." —unknown

place your photo here

_____ month

i like ... 15
_____
_____
_____

i like ... 16
_____
_____
_____

i like ... 17
_____
_____
_____

i like ... 18
_____
_____
_____

i like ... 19
_____
_____
_____

i like ... 20
_____
_____
_____

i like ... 21
_____
_____
_____

i like...ending the day knowing i did my best

_____ month

22 i like ...

23 i like ...

24 i like ...

25 i like ...

26 i like ...

27 i like ...

28 i like ...

i like…to be happy

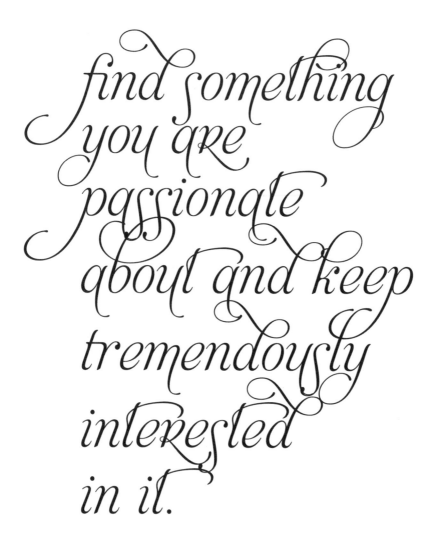

find something
you are
passionate
about and keep
tremendously
interested
in it.

-julia child

_____ month

i like ... **29** _____
_____
_____
_____

i like ... **30** _____
_____
_____
_____

i like ... **31** _____
_____
_____
_____

i like…trying something new

*do small things
with great love*
— mother teresa

_____ month

1   i like ...

2   i like ...

3   i like ...

4   i like ...

5   i like ...

6   i like ...

7   i like ...

i like…getting good news

month

i like ...
8

i like ...
9

i like ...
10

i like ...
11

i like ...
12

i like ...
13

i like ...
14

i like…singing out loud even when i don't know all the words

*"breathe in the freshness of the sea
breathe out the cares of the day"*

—annonymous

_____ month

i like ...
15

i like ...
16

i like ...
17

i like ...
18

i like ...
19

i like ...
20

i like ...
21

i like...warm rainy days

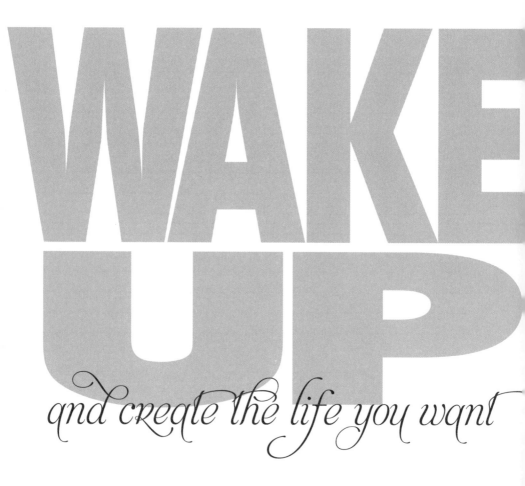

WAKE UP
and create the life you want

_____ month

i like ... **22**

i like ... **23**

i like ... **24**

i like ... **25**

i like ... **26**

i like ... **27**

i like ... **28**

i like…trying a new recipe

to be
true
you must
embrace
the life
that's
calling you...
and listen to
the whispers
in your soul

—unknown

_____ month

i like ... **29**
_____
_____
_____

i like ... **30**
_____
_____
_____

i like ... **31**
_____
_____
_____

i like...being active

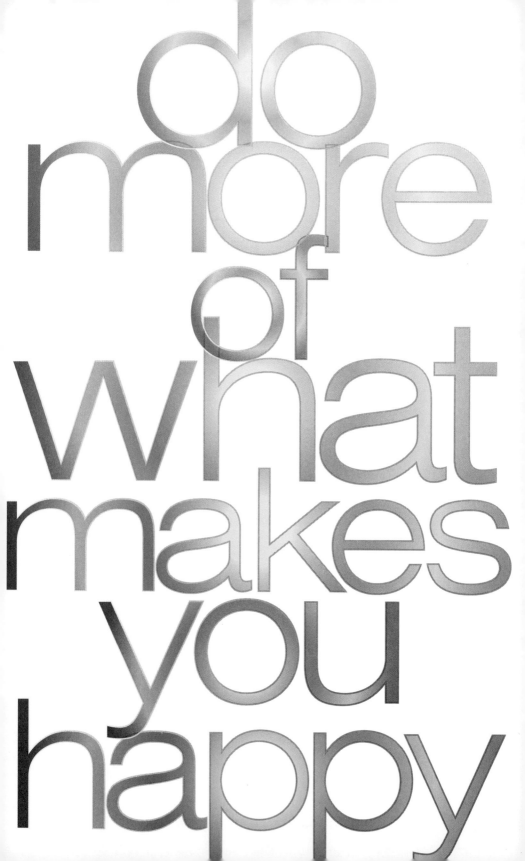

_____ month

1 i like ... _____

2 i like ... _____

3 i like ... _____

4 i like ... _____

5 i like ... _____

6 i like ... _____

7 i like ... _____

i like...bargain hunting

"if you obey all the rules, you'll miss all the fun."

—katherine hepburn

i like ... _____
8 _____
_____

i like ... _____
9 _____
_____

i like ... _____
10 _____
_____

i like ... _____
11 _____
_____

i like ... _____
12 _____
_____

i like ... _____
13 _____
_____

i like ... _____
14 _____
_____

i like...to travel

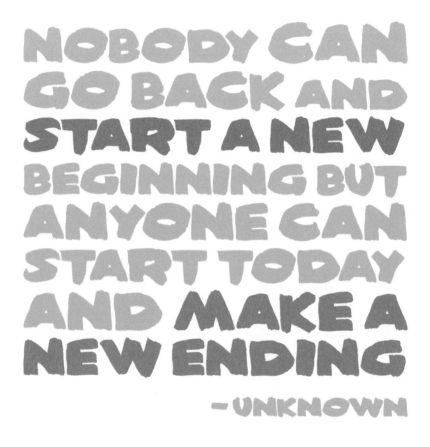

NOBODY CAN GO BACK AND START A NEW BEGINNING BUT ANYONE CAN START TODAY AND MAKE A NEW ENDING

— UNKNOWN

_____ month

i like ... _____
15 _____
_____

i like ... _____
16 _____
_____

i like ... _____
17 _____
_____

i like ... _____
18 _____
_____

i like ... _____
19 _____
_____

i like ... _____
20 _____
_____

i like ... _____
21 _____
_____

i like...to help others

"
a
woman
is an
amazing
being,
if only
she knew."
— meredith looney

month

i like ...
22

i like ...
23

i like ...
24

i like ...
25

i like ...
26

i like ...
27

i like ...
28

i like…to do random acts of kindness

_____ month

i like ...

29 _____
_____
_____
_____

i like ...

30 _____
_____
_____
_____

i like ...

31 _____
_____
_____
_____

i like...oversized handbags

you are incredible. *adorable*, lovable, wonderful *powerful*, perfectly *beautiful* just the way **you are**

_____ month

i like ... _____
1 _____
_____
_____

i like ... _____
2 _____
_____
_____

i like ... _____
3 _____
_____
_____

i like ... _____
4 _____
_____
_____

i like ... _____
5 _____
_____
_____

i like ... _____
6 _____
_____
_____

i like ... _____
7 _____
_____
_____

i like...to laugh out loud

_____ month

i like ... _____
8 _____
_____
_____

i like ... _____
9 _____
_____
_____

i like ... _____
10 _____
_____
_____

i like ... _____
11 _____
_____
_____

i like ... _____
12 _____
_____
_____

i like ... _____
13 _____
_____
_____

i like ... _____
14 _____
_____
_____

i like...making new friends

i just need
some time
in a
beautiful
place to
clear my
head

_____ month

i like ... _____
15 _____
_____
_____

i like ... _____
16 _____
_____
_____

i like ... _____
17 _____
_____
_____

i like ... _____
18 _____
_____
_____

i like ... _____
19 _____
_____
_____

i like ... _____
20 _____
_____
_____

i like ... _____
21 _____
_____
_____

i like...a good cry during a movie

"find out who you are
and do it on purpose."

-dolly parton

_____ month

i like ... 22

i like ... 23

i like ... 24

i like ... 25

i like ... 26

i like ... 27

i like ... 28

i like…to indulge in something delicious

the journey
of a thousand miles
begins with
one
step.

—lao-tzu

_____ month

i like ... **29** _____
_____
_____

i like ... **30** _____
_____
_____

i like ... **31** _____
_____
_____

i like...to be creative

live as an original

_____ month

1 i like ... _____
_____
_____
_____

2 i like ... _____
_____
_____
_____

3 i like ... _____
_____
_____
_____

4 i like ... _____
_____
_____
_____

5 i like ... _____
_____
_____
_____

6 i like ... _____
_____
_____
_____

7 i like ... _____
_____
_____
_____

i like...shopping for shoes

_____ month

i like ... _____
8 _____
_____
_____

i like ... _____
9 _____
_____
_____

i like ... _____
10 _____
_____
_____

i like ... _____
11 _____
_____
_____

i like ... _____
12 _____
_____
_____

i like ... _____
13 _____
_____
_____

i like ... _____
14 _____
_____
_____

i like...cheesecake

did you know...

there are 4 cars and 11 light posts on the back of a 10 dollar bill.

humming birds can't walk.

the fastest speed a falling raindrop can hit you is 18 mph.

human teeth are almost as hard as rocks.

bingo is the name of the dog on the cracker jack box.

women blink up to two times as much as men do.

the original name for the butterfly was flutterby.

it takes 17 muscles to smile and 43 to frown.

a jiffy is actually 1/100th of a second.

month

i like ... _____
15

i like ... _____
16

i like ... _____
17

i like ... _____
18

i like ... _____
19

i like ... _____
20

i like ... _____
21

i like...alone time

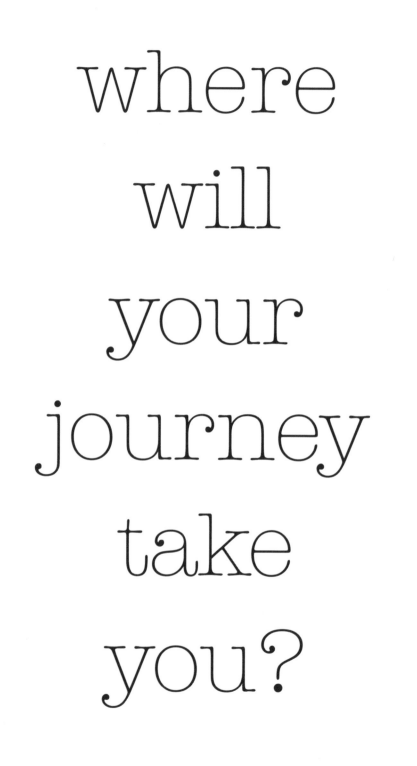

month

i like ... _____
22
_____
_____
_____

i like ... _____
23
_____
_____
_____

i like ... _____
24
_____
_____
_____

i like ... _____
25
_____
_____
_____

i like ... _____
26
_____
_____
_____

i like ... _____
27
_____
_____
_____

i like ... _____
28
_____
_____
_____

i like...going on vacation

"nothing is impossible,
the word itself says i'm possible!"

—audrey hepburn

_____ month

i like ... 29 _____
_____
_____
_____

i like ... 30 _____
_____
_____
_____

i like ... 31 _____
_____
_____
_____

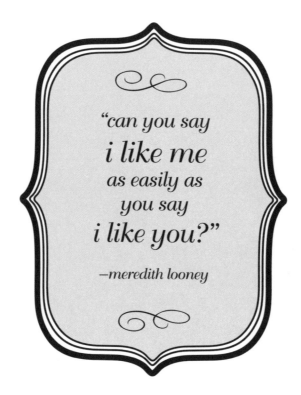

"can you say
i like me
as easily as
you say
i like you?"

—meredith looney

_____ month

i like ... _____
1 _____
_____
_____

i like ... _____
2 _____
_____
_____

i like ... _____
3 _____
_____
_____

i like ... _____
4 _____
_____
_____

i like ... _____
5 _____
_____
_____

i like ... _____
6 _____
_____
_____

i like ... _____
7 _____
_____
_____

i like...my life

_____ month

i like ... _____
8 _____
_____
_____

i like ... _____
9 _____
_____
_____

i like ... _____
10 _____
_____
_____

i like ... _____
11 _____
_____
_____

i like ... _____
12 _____
_____
_____

i like ... _____
13 _____
_____
_____

i like ... _____
14 _____
_____
_____

i like...cool sheets on a hot night

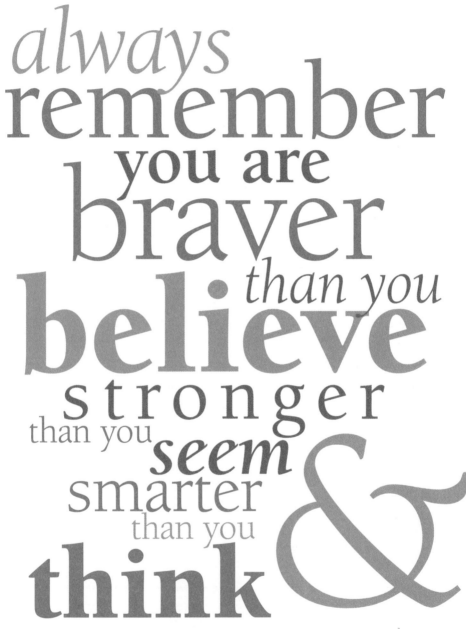

always
remember
you are
braver
than you
believe
stronger
than you *seem*
smarter
than you
think

—unknown

_____ month

i like ... **15** _____

i like ... **16** _____

i like ... **17** _____

i like ... **18** _____

i like ... **19** _____

i like ... **20** _____

i like ... **21** _____

i like...when the leaves begin to fall

"life is like ice cream *enjoy* it before it melts."

—*unknown*

_____ month

i like ... **22** _____
_____
_____
_____

i like ... **23** _____
_____
_____
_____

i like ... **24** _____
_____
_____
_____

i like ... **25** _____
_____
_____
_____

i like ... **26** _____
_____
_____
_____

i like ... **27** _____
_____
_____
_____

i like ... **28** _____
_____
_____
_____

i like…spending time with friends

be
your
own
kind of
beautiful

_____ month

i like ... **29**
_____
_____
_____
_____

i like ... **30**
_____
_____
_____
_____

i like ... **31**
_____
_____
_____
_____

i like…the sound of the ocean

"the best and
most beautiful things
in the world
cannot be seen or
even touched.
they must be felt
with the heart."

-helen keller

_____ month

1 i like ... _____
_____
_____
_____

2 i like ... _____
_____
_____
_____

3 i like ... _____
_____
_____
_____

4 i like ... _____
_____
_____
_____

5 i like ... _____
_____
_____
_____

6 i like ... _____
_____
_____
_____

7 i like ... _____
_____
_____
_____

i like...rainbows

happiness is like a butterfly
the more you chase it
the more it will elude you
but if you turn your attention
to other things it will come and
sit softly on your shoulder

_____ month

8 i like ...
_____
_____
_____

9 i like ...
_____
_____
_____

10 i like ...
_____
_____
_____

11 i like ...
_____
_____
_____

12 i like ...
_____
_____
_____

13 i like ...
_____
_____
_____

14 i like ...
_____
_____
_____

i like...looking through old photos

you is kind

you is smart

you is important

— aibileen clark

The Help by Kathryn Stockett

_____ month

i like ... **15** _____
_____
_____

i like ... **16** _____
_____
_____

i like ... **17** _____
_____
_____

i like ... **18** _____
_____
_____

i like ... **19** _____
_____
_____

i like ... **20** _____
_____

i like ... **21** _____
_____

i like...starry nights

"life is too short
kiss slowly
laugh insanely
love truly
and forgive quickly."

—unknown

_____ month

i like ... **22**
_____
_____
_____

i like ... **23**
_____
_____
_____

i like ... **24**
_____
_____
_____

i like ... **25**
_____
_____
_____

i like ... **26**
_____
_____
_____

i like ... **27**
_____
_____
_____

i like ... **28**
_____
_____
_____

i like…picking fresh flowers

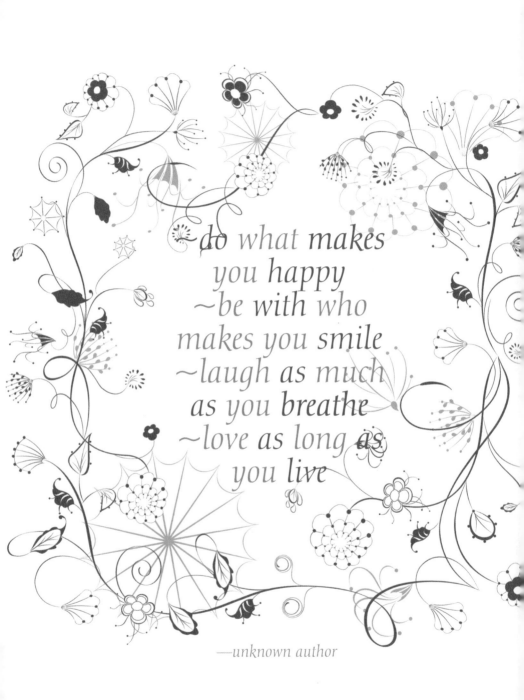

do what makes
you happy
~be with who
makes you smile
~laugh as much
as you breathe
~love as long as
you live

—unknown author

month

i like ... **29**

i like ... **30**

i like ... **31**

i like...peace and quiet

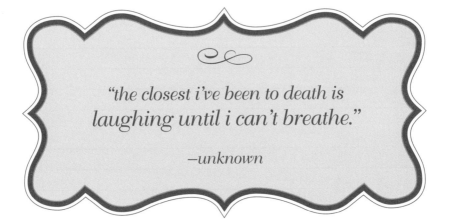

"the closest i've been to death is
laughing until i can't breathe."

—unknown

_____ month

i like ...
1 _____
_____
_____
_____

i like ...
2 _____
_____
_____
_____

i like ...
3 _____
_____
_____
_____

i like ...
4 _____
_____
_____
_____

i like ...
5 _____
_____
_____
_____

i like ...
6 _____
_____
_____
_____

i like ...
7 _____
_____
_____
_____

i like...staying busy and feeling productive

CLEAR YOUR HEAD
fill your soul

_____ month

i like ... _____
8 _____
_____
_____

i like ... _____
9 _____
_____
_____

i like ... _____
10 _____
_____
_____

i like ... _____
11 _____
_____
_____

i like ... _____
12 _____
_____
_____

i like ... _____
13 _____
_____
_____

i like ... _____
14 _____
_____
_____

i like...watching my favorite movie for the 100th time

my bucket list

_____

_____

_____

_____

_____

_____

_____

_____

_____

month

i like ... **15**

i like ... **16**

i like ... **17**

i like ... **18**

i like ... **19**

i like ... **20**

i like ... **21**

i like…good dreams

"learn to hear what your inner voice is telling you, and your whole world changes."

—oprah

_____ month

i like ...
22
_____
_____
_____

i like ...
23
_____
_____
_____

i like ...
24
_____
_____
_____

i like ...
25
_____
_____
_____

i like ...
26
_____
_____
_____

i like ...
27
_____
_____
_____

i like ...
28
_____
_____
_____

i like…to love and be loved

"live for the moments
you can't put into words."

—unknown

_____ month

i like ...

29

i like ...

30

i like ...

31

i like…the smell of fresh clean laundry

be the
type of
person
you want to
meet

—unknown

_____ month

1 i like ... _____
_____
_____

2 i like ... _____
_____
_____

3 i like ... _____
_____
_____

4 i like ... _____
_____
_____

5 i like ... _____
_____
_____

6 i like ... _____
_____
_____

7 i like ... _____
_____
_____

i like…springtime flowers

"keep a dream in your pocket and faith in your heart."

-unknown

_____ month

i like ... _____
8 _____
_____

i like ... _____
9 _____
_____

i like ... _____
10 _____
_____

i like ... _____
11 _____
_____

i like ... _____
12 _____
_____

i like ... _____
13 _____
_____

i like ... _____
14 _____
_____

i like...that i made someone feel special today

_____ month

i like ... 15

i like ... 16

i like ... 17

i like ... 18

i like ... 19

i like ... 20

i like ... 21

i like...music

"when life gives you a hundred
reasons to cry, show life that you
have a thousand reasons to smile."
— unknown

_____ month

i like ... **22** _____

i like ... **23** _____

i like ... **24** _____

i like ... **25** _____

i like ... **26** _____

i like ... **27** _____

i like ... **28** _____

i like…working hard to feel healthy

"life is a game, play it;

life is a challenge, meet it;

life is an opportunity, capture it."

—unknown

_____ month

i like ...
29
_____
_____
_____
_____

i like ...
30
_____
_____
_____
_____

i like ...
31
_____
_____
_____
_____

i like...to inspire others

"just when the caterpillar thought the world was over, it became a butterfly."

—anonymous

_____ month

i like ... _____
1 _____
_____
_____

i like ... _____
2 _____
_____
_____

i like ... _____
3 _____
_____
_____

i like ... _____
4 _____
_____
_____

i like ... _____
5 _____
_____
_____

i like ... _____
6 _____
_____
_____

i like ... _____
7 _____
_____
_____

i like…making a difference in the world

my proudest accomplishments are

_____ month

i like ... _____
8

i like ... _____
9

i like ... _____
10

i like ... _____
11

i like ... _____
12

i like ... _____
13

i like ... _____
14

i like...getting lost in a good book

"success is temporary
significance
is eternal"

—unknown

_____ month

i like ... 15

i like ... 16

i like ... 17

i like ... 18

i like ... 19

i like ... 20

i like ... 21

i like...romance

"there are no extra pieces in the universe. everyone is here because he or she has a place to fill and every piece must fit itself into the big jigsaw puzzle."

—deepak chopra

month

i like ... 22

i like ... 23

i like ... 24

i like ... 25

i like ... 26

i like ... 27

i like ... 28

i like...being silly

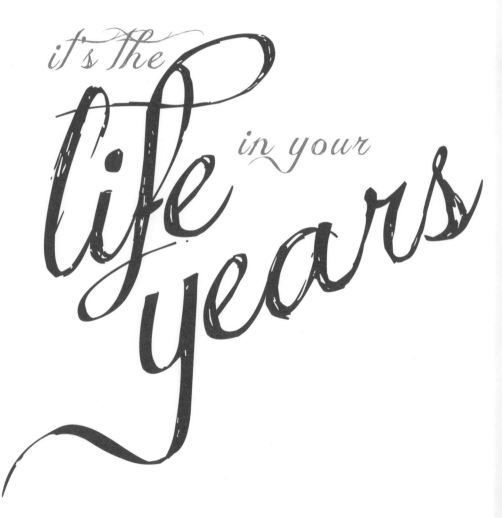

and in the end,
it's not the *years*
in your *life* that count.

it's the *life* in your *years*

_____ month

i like ... 29
_____
_____
_____
_____

i like ... 30
_____
_____
_____
_____

i like ... 31
_____
_____
_____
_____

i like…dancing

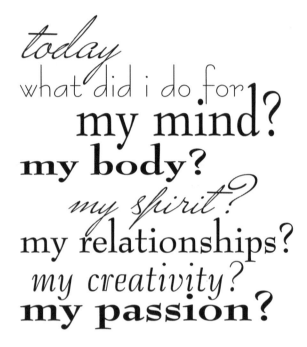

today
what did i do for
my mind?
my body?
my spirit?
my relationships?
my creativity?
my passion?

_____ month

1 i like ... _____
_____
_____

2 i like ... _____
_____
_____

3 i like ... _____
_____
_____

4 i like ... _____
_____
_____

5 i like ... _____
_____
_____

6 i like ... _____
_____
_____

7 i like ... _____
_____
_____

i like...getting dressed up for no reason

be *nice*
to yourself.
it's hard to be **happy**

when *someone's* mean to you all the *time.*

—unknown

i like ...
8

i like ...
9

i like ...
10

i like ...
11

i like ...
12

i like ...
13

i like ...
14

i like...long walks

"there is *more* to *life* than *increasing* the speed."

—gandhi

_____ month

i like ... **15**
_____
_____
_____

i like ... **16**
_____
_____
_____

i like ... **17**
_____
_____
_____

i like ... **18**
_____
_____
_____

i like ... **19**
_____
_____
_____

i like ... **20**
_____
_____
_____

i like ... **21**
_____
_____
_____

i like...the sunshine on my face

"you can't learn from remembering, you can't learn from guessing. you can only learn from moving forward at the rate you are moved, as brightness into brightness."

-sarah manguso

_____ month

i like ... _____
22

i like ... _____
23

i like ... _____
24

i like ... _____
25

i like ... _____
26

i like ... _____
27

i like ... _____
28

i like…knowing i'm the best me i can be

"enjoy the little things in life,
for one day you may look back
and realize they we the big things."

—unknown

_____ month

i like ...
29
_____
_____
_____
_____

i like ...
30
_____
_____
_____
_____

i like ...
31
_____
_____
_____
_____

i like...the new confident me

"write your own *happily ever after.*"
—unknown

place your photo here

notes & thoughts

notes & thoughts

notes & thoughts

live your life

notes & thoughts

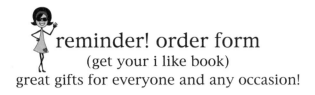

reminder! order form
(get your i like book)
great gifts for everyone and any occasion!

send books to:

_____
name/company

_____
street address

_____
city   state   zip

e-mail _____

contact phone (_____)_____

i like book for couples, please indicate number of copies _____

i like book for kids, please indicate number of copies for:
blue (_____) pink (_____) purple (_____) green (_____)
orange (_____) red (_____)

i like book for women, please indicate number of copies _____

i like you, i really do, please indicate number of copies _____

please visit www.theilikebook.com for pricing.

payment method:

_____ check/money order
(please make checks payable to: Lucky Looney LLC)

please send order form with check/money order to:
the i like book
p.o. box 4091
parker, co. 80134

all credit card and paypal orders can be made at www.theilikebook.com

comments_____
_____
_____

contact: the i like book—p.o. box 4091, parker co 80134
tel: (888)737-like   www.theilikebook.com

about meredith

meredith looney is an author and entrepreneur whose passion is strengthening relationships with her groundbreaking collection of i like books. she has a special gift of creating products for helping people see the best in themselves and others through her back to the basics philosophy of daily likes. a graduate of texas state university, meredith now lives in denver, colorado with her husband and two children.